Find the pairs

Find the stickers and put them in place. Look at the picture and find
the pairs of roller boots. Draw lines to ma

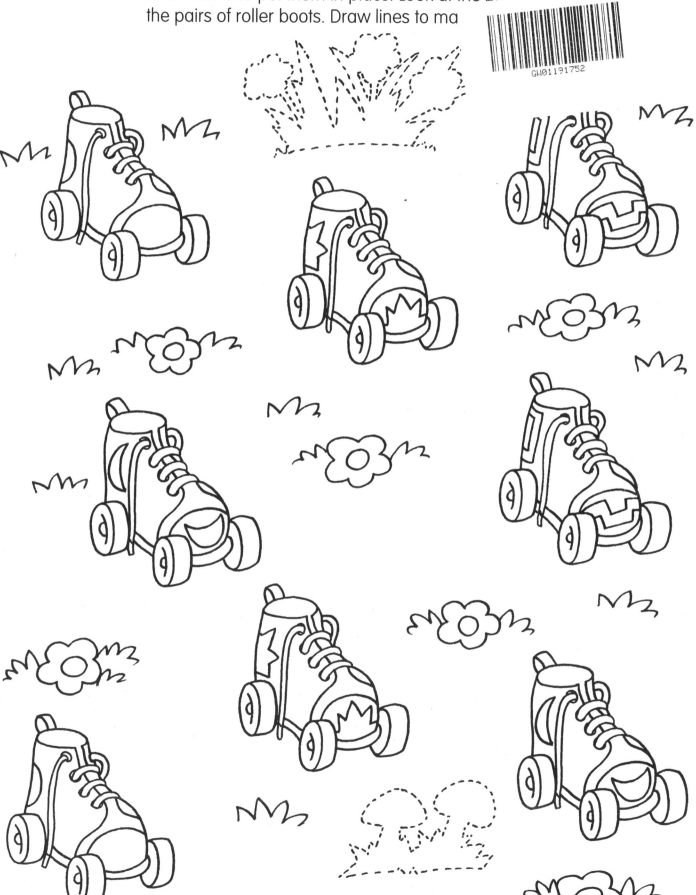

In the town

Find the stickers and put them in place. Look carefully at the picture and find 40 wheels.

REPAIRS

George
the Grocer

At the seaside

Find the stickers and put them in place.
Look carefully at the picture and find 58 triangles.

Find and count

Find the stickers and put them in place.
Look carefully at the picture and find 80 windows.

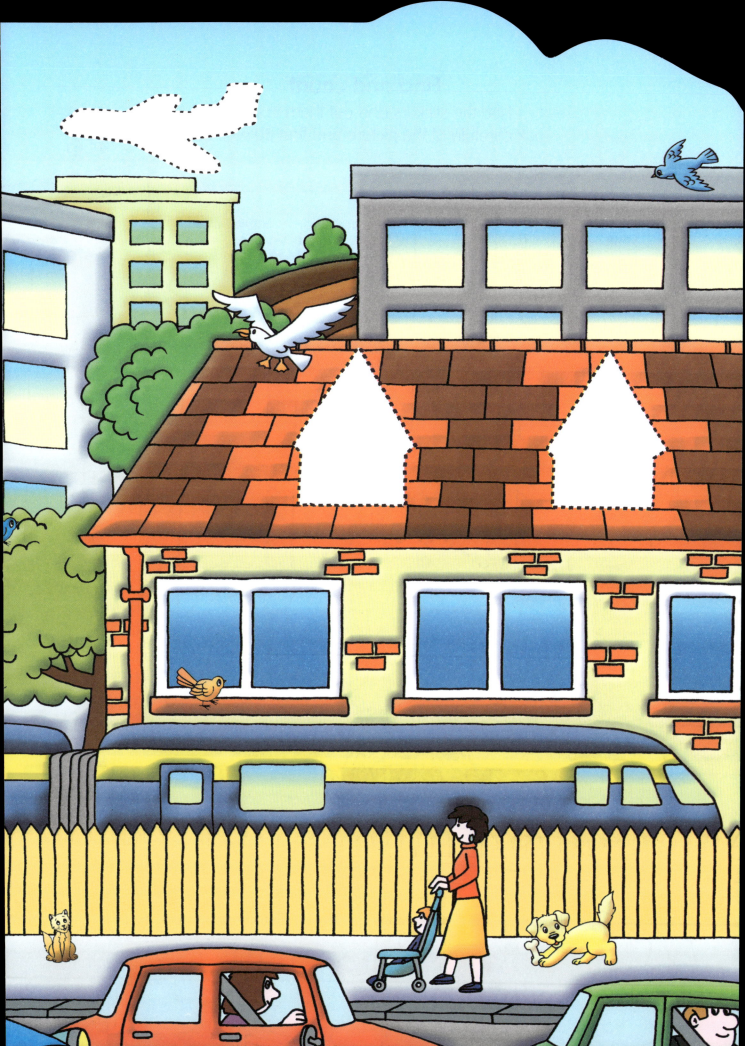

Fun in the snow

Find the stickers and put them in place.
Look carefully at the picture and find 20 hats.

seat

handlebars

tank

backlight

exhaust

brake

headlight

mudguard

wheel

number-plate

What goes where?

Find the stickers to name the different parts
of a motorbike.

Where's that wheel?

Find the stickers and put them in place.
Look carefully at the picture and find out where the wheels belong.
Draw lines to join the wheels to the right vehicles.

Safety first

Find the stickers and put them in place. Look at the picture and draw lines to join the person to the safety gear.

a   b   c   d

Who rides what?

Find the stickers and put them in place. Look at the picture carefully and draw lines to join the rider to the bike.

Parking places

Find the stickers and put them in place. Look carefully at the picture and find 30 headlights. Draw steering wheels and drivers in the vehicles. Make up some number-plates.

MIXIT

blooms

Transport crossword

Find the stickers and put them in place.
The pictures are clues and the numbers show where each word goes.
Write the words in the grid.

Safety first

a. racing car driver
b. boy
c. motorbike rider
d. tractor driver

Answers

Who rides what?

1. pennyfarthing
2. tandem
3. tricycle
4. mountain bike
5. racing bike

Transport crossword

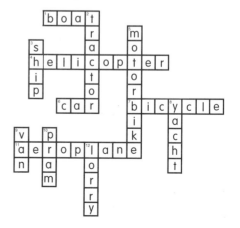